Making

MAKING MIRRORS

Writing/Righting
by and for **Refugees**

EDITED BY **JEHAN BSEISO** AND **BECKY THOMPSON**

OLIVE
BRANCH
PRESS

An imprint of Interlink Publishing Group, Inc.
www.interlinkbooks.com

First published in 2019 by

OLIVE BRANCH PRESS
An imprint of Interlink Publishing Group, Inc.
46 Crosby Street
Northampton, MA 01060
www.interlinkbooks.com

"My People's Story," by Ibtisam Barakat was previously published in *Balcony on the Moon: Coming of Age in Palestine* (New York: Macmillan Publishing Group, Farrar, Straus, and Giroux Books for Young Readers, 2016). Reprinted by permission.

Library of Congress Cataloging-in-Publication data available:
ISBN-13: 978-1-62371-978-4

Printed and bound in the United States of America

To the families and lovers at the bottom of the sea

Contents

Is Home My Ghost?

Nazim Hikmet

Excerpt from

"Some Advice for Those Who Will Serve Time in Prison"

(1949)

To think of roses and gardens inside is bad,
to think of seas and mountains is good.
Read and write without rest,
and I also advise weaving
and making mirrors
I mean, it's not that you can't pass
      ten or fifteen years inside
              and more—
        you can,
        as long as the jewel
        on the left side of your chest doesn't lose its luster!

Nathalie Handal

Heartsong

Only they saw the waves
Only they saw the wind
as the houses collapsed
Only they dreamt of dreams
There were no birds
There were no trees
No hands to cover their eyes
No rain to record their footsteps
Only they saw their photos fading
into the walls
Only they saw their stories
hidden in the sounds of strangers
Only they
they stayed to tell us
they were never gone
they lay in their shadows
guarding their origin
their heart in every note
of every song
they stayed to tell us
there will always be
a heart in the sea
with our names

Preface

by Becky Thompson and Jehan Bseiso

Making Mirrors is a collection of poetry by and for refugees that began on two continents, envisioned by Palestinian poet and aid worker, Jehan Bseiso, and Becky Thompson, a US-based poet and professor changed by months of witnessing Syrians, Pakistanis, Palestinians, Eritreans, Iraqis, and Afghans survive their perilous journey across the Aegean Sea. For Turkish political prisoner and poet Nazim Hikmet, "making mirrors" is an active verb and a plural noun, it is also a tool of resistance he offers up for "those who will serve time in prison." In this collection we make mirrors to reflect imagistic connections that allow us to see ourselves in each other, those on rafts and those standing on the shore, those waiting/writing in detention and those writing from places of relative safety, those who lift their children to the sky and those whose bodies are at the bottom of the sea.

From a Beirut café in 2016, Jehan and Becky put out a call for submissions to poets who immediately sent essential, daunting poems. These poets then reached out to other poets, sometimes translating their poetry so they could submit too. From the start we wanted to create a space for writers to share their work and to include refugee poets on the move. To make this possible, Becky Thompson taught poetry workshops in several "camps" in Greece. This process allowed us to include poets currently risking their lives to save their lives. Among them is Fatma Al Hassan, a mother of eight who taped paintings and poetry on the walls of her cubicle in Elpida, a center for vulnerable families in Thessaloniki, Greece during the eighteen months she waited in limbo with her children. "In the Belly of the Sea" was written by a young Iranian father, Abbas Sheikhi who met Becky at a poetry workshop she offered at Khora, a refugee center in the heart of Athens.

Nisreen Aj's words first came to us via Facebook, a few months after Becky met her in Mytilini. At nineteen Aj traveled with her fourteen-year-old brother from Syria to Greece, telling Becky that she was no poet, her major in college, molecular biology, even as she sketched beautiful lines on scrap paper. Since 2016 we have not been able to find her—and two other people whose poems we hoped to include in this volume—Nawwar Kamal Al Hassani and Ahmed Qaisania. Their absence is present. Sadly we cannot include Nisreen Aj's poem without her written permission, but we can share her words here: "I love a bird's life, holding in its wings all of the world. It doesn't know the meaning of borders. It takes the trees as its home, doesn't hate. There are words without letters. There is heart without pulsations. There are eyes without insight. There are people without country. There is country without people. But, there is no life without mother."

The poems in *Making Mirrors* show us that the term "refugee" is, itself, precarious. It also contains multitudes. The poet Fady Joudah recently wrote to us cautioning against generalizing the experience of displacement, "the perpetuation of images [of refugees] is so intense, and so entrapped in its own limitations toward justice and action and witness that its effect has become fixed, predictable. There has to be other ways." Our work then, as editors, has been to seek poems that search for those other ways by offering words that go beyond refugee/citizen binaries, that illuminate exile as a forced/creative space, that move us beyond witnessing that "encodes its own automatism." We find specificity in the words of Sharif Elmusa, "I want my house to stand. / I want the walls back / To weep alone / To hang pictures."

In many of the poems we see ghosts in the mirrors haunted by conscience and memory. In "The World Grows Blackhorn Walls," Iranian-born poet and translator Sholeh Wolpé asks, "is home my ghost? // Does it wear my underwear / folded neatly in the antique chest / of drawers I bought twenty years ago? // Is it lost between the lines of books / shelved alphabetical in a language / I was not born to?" With this haunting, a witness presence often steps in, not always friendly, sometimes disturbing, sometimes wise. In Mohsen Emadi's "It is snowing outside..." a dead bird is a witness presence: "Your body is a bird. My love is a dead bird...I, in the hour of ghosts, jumped out of your sleep. My body is a dead bird."

The poets in *Making Mirrors* ask the question, How can we remember what we can't forget? In Omar Alsayyed's poem "Misplaced Home" the poet explains, "The ghosts moved away...And no one's left to look back into my eyes." Wolpé teaches us that, to be in touch with ghosts is to "know what it's like to be an outsider /// But mark this—I do not belong anywhere. / I have an accent in every language I speak." In Sinan Antoon's "Afterwords," return is not only possible, it is inevitable after death. Mohja Kahf makes a grim and broken mirror reflect Leonard Cohen's "Who by Fire" in order to reveal "Who by sarin gas, who by militia knife." To know ghosts, to write with a witness presence, is to claim outsider status, as resistance, as tradition.

Whether physically imprisoned, barred from returning home, or caught in traumatic memory the poets caution against complacency. Lebanese poet Zeina Hashem Beck writes, "Remember / the name your parents gave you / has plenty of shade." Here, we see deep resonance with Nazim Hikmet's advice, "It's not that you can't pass / ten or fifteen years inside / and more— / you can, / as long as the jewel / on the left side of your chest doesn't lose its luster!" From the Balkan route to deportation, the poet Khaled Mattawa's cycle poems are located "between privilege and pity / a paradise of tolerable solitude / a checkpoint at a hope that slides." Many of the poems retreat from the horror of reality into the sanctuary of that jewel, the heart, even if the respite is brief. Lena Khalaf Tuffaha writes that "The forecast calls for white phosphorus / with occasional sunbreaks" reminding us that terror is woven into war's weather patterns. For Fadwa Suleiman absurdity becomes a titrated scream as "half of you will be slaughtered by the other half / And the sky has locked its doors."

Amidst this terror, resilience fights back as Beck writes, "I will make love / to you in a bed of blood and faith," letting us know sensuality still finds its way into lovers' lives, even in detention centers and refugee camps. Saad Abdullah speaks out: "Don't kill the lovestruck stars." In "Squatters' Rights," LGBT refugees from multiple countries occupy a building in Athens for a late night party, traditional dancing interwoven with rock 'n' roll's bump and grind "as the base of the sound system / hijacks old fear....community / traveling with tattoos and silk scarves." Beck closes her gorgeous poem with: "kiss me, for where else / do we carry home now, *habibi*, / if not on our lips?" There is always love and hope even if the Mediterranean crossing is deadly and dangerous, and for Naomi Shihab Nye the sea is "too wide for comfort, and nowhere to receive a letter for a very long time."

Habeebi, a quintessential term of endearment, is also a name for survival as in "Habeebi, just take the boat."

As the refugee crisis fades from the front page of newspapers and refugee voices are drowned out by other horrors of breaking news around the world, from political stalemates to climate change, *Making Mirrors* is a plea against historical amnesia and its twin, psychic inertia. In this way, *Mirrors* is an antidote that reaches beyond despair to renewed action. Wolpé teaches, "Why do they call us *alien* / as if we come from other planets? // I carry seeds in my mouth, plant / turmeric, cardamom, and tiny / aromatic cucumbers in this garden... They will grow, I know, against / these blackthorn walls. They are magic."

The number of people forced to flee their homes, 65 million, is the largest one ever recorded. In this climate of supposed compassion fatigue, *Making Mirrors* offers a poetics of belonging—to the earth, to family, to each other, to countries set on fire and to memories packed into backpacks. Ruth Awad writes, "I carry these suitcases full of rain / because I can't take my country./ If it's a choice you want—I've never known / a world that wasn't worth dying for."

This is an anthology written by refugees at the center of this crisis. These poems reveal that diaspora is complicated and unsettling; becoming a refugee is an experience that is impossible to locate on a map, yet seared into consciousness. The nineteen-year-old poet Sara Abou Rashed living in the US writes, "I, too yearn for peace, because I drop poems, not bombs." The twenty-year-old Baha' Ebdeir living in Bethlehem writes, "But wait! Was I actually destined to be born occupied? Again, I don't dream of freedom. I see myself free."

Acknowledgements

Thank you to all of the poets who trusted us with your poems, our talisman.

To all the people who let me (Becky) walk with you, day after day, in 2015–2016. I sit here now, in Lesvos Greece, sending these poems to you from the same place I used to slip out from in the early morning to meet rafts. I can see Turkey from here, only now there is a huge gray warship in the tiny sliver of sea between Turkey and Lesvos.

To all the poets who risked writing in "Love Calls Us to the Things of This World" poetry workshops in refugee camps in Greece. To all those who led us to them—Jumana Abo Oxa, Michael Kazan, Samer Better, Eric and Philippa Kempson. To the Joinda family, your music and videos reverberate across the world.

For guiding *Making Mirrors* into the world, thank you to Lisa Majaj, Sholeh Wolpé, Naomi Shihab Nye, Marilyn Hacker, Sharif Elmusa, Ibtisam Barakat, Fred Marchant, Marcia Lynx Qualey, and Susan Kosoff. To Ethelbert Miller, Kathy Engel, and Kamal Boullata, who came before, teaching us, we begin here. To Randall Horton, your eye, your heart. To Diane Harriford, scanning the sea together.

To Zenaida Peterson, Emily Wilson, and Christy Choueiri, for expert technical skills. To Mootacem Bellah Mhiri, Marilyn Hacker, and Lyn Coffin for stellar translations.

To Michel Moushabeck, Pam Fontes-May, Whitney Sanderson, and all of the people at Interlink, for whom publishing is a way of living.

For all our mothers and fathers. For Musallam, Hamza, Jehan, Arifa, Darwish and Inas Bseiso and all those forced out from their homes and their lands. To Edward and Sally Abood, for teaching how poems are like birds—fierce, fragile, long-distance fliers.

Fadwa Suleiman, your courage is present to us, still.

HABEEBI,
JUST TAKE THE BOAT

Abbas Sheikhi

In the Belly of the Sea

We were in a boat
we were afraid of the darkness
the waves sent us to the sky
and the sky cried for us
women were crying
and men were praying
I prayed but didn't cry
because of my small daughter
our son in my wife's belly
whispered to us, don't worry
the sea calmed down
God's eye saw us.

Becky Thompson

Splitting/siblings

as ancient
as the
sun
losing
its moon
on auction
blocks
the oldest
to the highest
bidder
now in Moria
detention/center/one
brother
granted/asylum
the/younger
deported.
Shall
we/draw
each other
on our
bodies?
Sing/praises
to/ an absent
god?
Refuse to
write
rhyme/ reason?
Progress, a line/
stuck on/
pause?

Fady Joudah

An Algebra Come Home

Morning slept well. The fruit vendor, in a Paris street market whose name I can access but don't recall, the immigrant sliced his heart like a peach, a plum, and called out to passersby, city dwellers, tourists to try this heart of his, not too sour not too sweet, ripe, ready, his bare hands looked as dry as can be expected, the pocket knife blade clean as well. So many refused, only a few reached out and let his quartered peach fall unto their fingertips like a flower furling, ate it then walked off with or without shaking their heads: No thank you or Yes but No. You chewed and then picked four fruits, one for each chamber. And he said "Beautiful, you're the one who's mended my heart."

Baha' Ebdeir
The key of return:

As I entered the gate of Ayda Camp, there was a large statue of a key at the top of a gate. They call it the key of return. It is so huge and is a metallic gray color. Every time I see someone entering the gate, I start thinking of the possibility that this key of return might fall down on one of those many people coming in and out. It is so unfair and annoying when your freedom is hung up at the top of a gate. It is so high that you cannot reach it, touch it, or even know what it smells like.

I have seen the children in the camp climbing the steel pillars and the walls, but I have never seen any of them climbing the gate in order to reach out to the huge key of return. It has crossed my mind that if we cannot touch a piece of metal representing the right of freedom and return, then how can we still hope to have our right of freedom and return signed on an official paper. Young Basil climbed up the gate and embraced the huge key of return so tightly. It was not until he touched and embraced the key of return that I started believing again in freedom. Basil hung up the Palestinian flag at the top of the gate. The Palestinian flag was dancing to the sound of the wind. It was not just waving, but singing to those who were standing below the gate. The people of the camp were cheering for Basil, calling him fearless and free.

Childhood memories:
Please don't call me Mr. Ayda camp because I am not only a place for people to camp. I am a place where the street becomes a playground. Where children can't afford going to a fancy gym, so they climb the metal pillars and jump over the high walls instead. You can see the children playing football with their slippers. Boots and sneakers aren't actually their type. A child carelessly plays in his underwear. Another one walks through the streets barefoot. He falls to the ground, looks like he wants to cry, but holds back his tears and smiles instead.

Children play with rocks instead of a Nike ball.

I am a circus where you can see children spinning broken tires. Where kites are made from plastic bags. No matter how high the kite flies, it always ends up getting stuck in the barbed wire fence. But still, that doesn't stop them from flying more and more kites. I am an adventurous experience and a risky life.

Basil and Sarah were young children playing hide-and-seek together. You could hear their laughter and screaming in every corner of the street. Sarah is all grown up now, she wears Hijab, she doesn't talk to guys. She walked by Basil's grocery the other day, but couldn't look him in the eye. He wanted to become a young child again, so he would grab her by the arm and be her superman. He wanted her to smile back at him when he smiled. Now, the camp is no longer their playground, but a prison that imprisons their emotions. Neither the camp nor the people can tolerate their spontaneous smiles and loud screams anymore.

Delusional freedom:
They called me a refugee, a stranger, and an outsider. But still, I don't dream of freedom; I see myself free, because I have chosen to see that. Speaking of Freedom. It is nothing but birds, sunsets, and a flapping flag. I want to get accepted to such-and-such universities not because I am occupied, oppressed, or less privileged. I want you to accept me for my potential, dreams, and thoughtfulness. Let those be the most contributing factors in getting accepted to your privileged universities. I am tired of humanizing myself, so I can get prioritized over other humans applying for the same scholarship, position, and job. Peace runs through my blood; you don't have to ask me controversial questions that could trigger me and trick me into saying bad stuff about my occupier. I want to make peace, but I will not settle for something less than I deserve. My Freedom is non-negotiable, my dignity is inalienable, and what is mine is mine. I am honored that you are discriminating against me for my beloved nationality and religion. I know, my name might be too Arab ... Fatima, Ahmad, and Ali altogether forming my full name. Yeah, I am not John, Alex, or even Paul. Was it my last name that got me stopped at every airport for hours? Was it my nationality that caused me to be underpaid? I am not a case study. I eat, I drink, and sleep like any other human.

The only difference is that I am a challenging human who couldn't challenge his destiny. But wait! Was I actually destined to be born occupied? Again, I don't dream of freedom; I see myself free, because I have chosen to see that.

Mohsen Emadi

It is snowing outside…

I

It is snowing outside. I'm listening to a song. Twice in this song I've
fallen in love. I don't know what language the song is in. It makes
no difference because I dream in one language and I fall in love in
another. Last year, I changed my residence five times. Last year, on
the stairs in my building, I saw a dead bird. I was afraid to bury her.
Maybe the woman who cleaned the building threw the bird away,
but for a whole year, I have been burying her in different countries.
This is absolute egoism on my part. Burying a dead bird doesn't affect
the bird, it just saves me having to watch her decay. But why should
I be afraid of decay? I, who lived through the longest war of the last
century and who fell in love a few years after the dictator died, I who
in later years preferred displacement to the next dictator. The fear of
decay can't be the same as the fear of death. It also does not depend
on location. It more closely resembles the fear of ugliness. Burial is
a matter of aesthetics. But aesthetics just opens a discussion about
the necessity or non-necessity of burying the bird and does not say
anything about my fear. It doesn't mention I was afraid to touch the
bird, even though I had touched several dead people. Some even died
in my arms. Also sometimes I doubt whether I'm still alive. This is
not strange for someone who falls asleep in one city and wakes up
in another city. Perhaps I was afraid I would catch something if I
touched the dead body of the bird. Maybe I was motivated by fear of
the unknown and—Well, no similarity or parallel to something makes
something else reasonable. The fact I was mostly not afraid to experi-
ence the unknown cannot provide a reason. Weak induction is usually
dangerous. With weak induction, the mystery is lost and the poetry
dies. It is therefore better for me to stop this and go back to looking
outside. It is still snowing and I do not dare listen to another song.

II

We always fall in love in the language of the country most recently
victorious. In the language of the victorious, we write elegies for the
defeated who have not yet been buried. I don't know why I can't sleep

at night. Last year, I worked in a restaurant at night, cleaning the toilets. Everybody left and my job started. One toilet stall was locked from the inside. With a spare key, I unlocked the stall and opened it. A drunk girl was sleeping there. I woke her up and brought her coffee. In an unknown language, she talked and cried. She was drunk and unable to understand the language of the victorious. I don't know why, instead of the warmth of her skin or the sorrow in her eyes or the thirst of her crying, I thought about the bombardment. Who am I to consider her characteristics? Was I measuring her with myself or independently? Her body that night was without a history. So why did I have to read her into my history? Could I have wanted to conquer her or let her conquer me? Anyway, her body cannot be the subject for negotiating about the bombardment. What if, when she was drinking her coffee, I was sitting closer to her? What if I was crying too? It was dawn when both of us left by the same door. I did not dare to touch her. Her body was alive. I don't know whether this fear came from the unknown or death. Perhaps both. But every midnight, next to the door of my toilet, my heart beat faster and there was nobody in there.

III

Your body is a bird. My love is a dead bird. What is similar about the body and the bird? Do I want to relate two fears? Which is more important—recognizing their similarity or understanding each of them? Why do I insist on seeing the two fears as equivalent to each other? Why do I borrow your body to make this comparison? Who benefits from this metaphor? A living bird does not cry for a dead bird. But why now, when it is dawn, do I occupy myself with this duality? Perhaps because nobody signed the order to bombard during the day? But many are being killed on the stairs or in the toilet. This song cries for something. Maybe for this reason, I fell in love in it. I don't know. You haven't heard this song. I can not know the bird's opinion. But I understand the crying of my body. In this song, in this place on the paper, passengers are going to their offices and a girl is facing the window, is drinking her last coffee. I, in the hour of ghosts, jumped out of your sleep. My body is a dead bird.

Translated from Persian by Lyn Coffin

Abu Bakr Khaal

Migrant Boat

We were
On a nameless
And lightless boat
The moon
Was casting
An insolent gaze
Dispassionate
And cold...
And the wind was unruly
As if ascending
From an abyss
Amidst the ridges
The boat was
Splintering
And disintegrating
Above
The water who was
Imbibing women, men
And children
Women were plunging
And never resurfacing...
And the men
Were stranded
On the surface of the water
Before disappearing...
Children's voices
Floated for a while
Before they died
I was floating
On a wooden board
Fighting the fury
Panting
For a breath
Of air

But the water
Was filling my nostrils
Not very far from me
Where the eye can see
There was a woman
Upon whom feasted the fish
Gnawing
Her breasts for milk and honey...
And the whirlwinds around me
I thought...were steeds...aloof
They took me by surprise
Their hooves...
Hefty...trotting
They were...
And I was
Panting for a breath
Of air
But...
Now the sand beat is nearing
The end
And the whirlwinds around me
Like nooses
Or steeds
Are pulling me down
With their
Cold hooves
Unstirred by the tremor
Of the ocean
And the agitation of the fish.

Translated from Arabic by Mootacem Bellah Mhiri

Naomi Shihab Nye

Mediterranean Blue

If you are the child of a refugee, you do not
sleep easily when they are crossing the sea
on small rafts and you know they can't swim.
My father couldn't swim either. He swam through
sorrow, though, and made it to the other side
on a ship, pitching his old clothes overboard
at landing, then tried to be happy, make a new life.
But something inside him was always paddling home,
clinging to anything that floated—a story, a food or face.
They are the bravest people on earth right now,
don't dare look down on them. Each mind a universe
swirling as many details as yours, as much love
for a humble place. Now the shirt is torn,
the sea too wide for comfort, and nowhere
to receive a letter for a very long time.

And if we can reach out a hand, we better.

Jehan Bseiso

No Search, No Rescue

I.
How do we overcome war and poverty only to drown in your sea?

II.
Misrata, Libya
Habeebi just take the boat.
In front of you : Bahr.
Behind you: Harb.
And the border, closed.
Your Sea, Mare, Bahr. Our war, our Harb.

III.
Augusta, Italy
Where is the interpreter?
This is my family.
Baba, mama, baby all washed up on the shore. This is 28 shoeless
survivors and thousands of bodies.
Bodies Syrian, Bodies Somali, Bodies Afghan, Bodies Ethiopian,
Bodies Eritrean.
Bodies Palestinian.
Your Sea, Mare, Bahr. Our war, our Harb.

IV.
Alexandria, Egypt
Habeebi, just take the boat.
Behind you Aleppo and Asmara, barrel bombs and Kalashnikovs.
In front of you a little bit of hope.
Your Sea, Mare, Bahr. Our war, our Harb.

V.
Maps on our backs.
Long way from home.

VILLAGES
HAVE NAMES TOO

Zeina Azzam

Leaving My Childhood Home

On our last day in Beirut
with my ten years packed in a suitcase,
my best friend asked for a keepsake.
I found a little tin box
to give her, emptied of lemon drops,
that would hold memories of our childhood:
us swinging in the dusty school yard,
rooftop hide and seek,
wispy-sweet jasmine, kilos
of summertime figs, King
of Falafel's tahini-bathed sandwiches,
our pastel autograph books.
All those remembrances
crammed in that box,
tiny storytellers waiting to speak.
Later her family would uproot too,
transplant like surly Palestinian weeds
pulled every few years.
We all knew about this,
even the kids.
I never saw her again
but know that she also
learned to travel lightly,
hauling empty boxes
pulsing with kilos
of memories.

Zeina Azzam

Colors for the Diaspora

Blue-green watery globe
tugging to a red core
we are a distant comet,
white cloud of unburnished rocks,
frisking the heavens
for an arc
to earth, sea, home.

Green-brown Palestine,
cactus fruit and wild thyme,
olive orchards, cypress trees...
we travel on your mountain tops
tethered by voices from suitcases
and the yaw of blackened keys.

Blue-black night
silver stars of ancestors
traveling a displaced orbit
around a lost sun, repeating:
when will we see the colors of our land,
when will we land....

Fadwa Suleiman

From Genesis

Rain on rain
And mud on mud
My grandmother weaves the story
With a thread of sun
And a thread of moon
She grinds her words
In the mill of her breath, and scatters them
Among the stars

     **

Rain on rain
And mud on clay
My grandmother turns with the earth
And kneads sand into her wine
At moonrise

     **

Rain on rain
And mud on mud
She attaches the sea to a pen
And spreads its breath on a page
She dries the salt on her knees
Gives birth to clouds
She makes fountains of her breasts
Gives birth to the grass

     **

Rain on rain
And mud on clay
At night my grandmother sows cities
That grow at daybreak
And she sings to the reeds

     **

Rain on rain
He writes on the clay
We have taken the one in the sky as our witness
And he said
The sky comes from you
The sky is for you
My grandmother locked
All the doors with the cry of her blood

      **

Rain on rain
And the clay tablets say
We have taken the one in the sky as our witness
He asked for blood
And would not accept our harvests
My grandmother barricaded
The doors with the cry of her blood

      **

Rain on rain
Blood on the grass
And grass above the blood
Blood leads to blood
Half of you will be slaughtered by the other half
And the sky has locked its doors

      **

Rain on rain
And mud on mud
She bends her neck to the wind
And her waist to the trunk of a fruit-tree
Bends her knees to the pebbles
And her forehead to the dust
She offers her fingers to the bees
And her teeth to the truth
Her songs to the reeds
And her feet to the roots
Her blood to the wedding of seed and flower
She lets her hair down over the story

**

Rain on rain
And mud on clay
My grandmother sets her fingers on fire waiting
For a prodigal to return
She gives off an odor of blood
My grandmother is still a virgin

**

Rain on rain
And mud on mud
Each time a herd of gazelles goes by
They are devoured by hunters
Who already had eaten their fill

**

Salt on a wound
And water on mud
We are only memories
In flight across time

Translated from Arabic by Marilyn Hacker

Ruth Awad

My Father Is the Sea, the Field, the Stone

I don't know what makes a country a country.
If the sea softening an edge of land is enough
to say, this is mine and that is yours.

There were nights in Tripoli
when there was room for us.
When the sky pulled up the wings of gulls

and we watched their bodies rise from the beach.
Days when I chased my sisters through the market
and we sailed through bright saffron scarves,

past barrels of grain and earthy bins of pine nuts.
And how I stood beside my siblings, all dressed
in clothes my father made stitch by stitch,

and held out my hands for the candy he'd bring
if work was good. I knew it was a lot to ask
and still I asked. Some days I'd swim out

until I wasn't sure I could come back.
The sun beat its indifference into my brow.
The water, its mercy. Why choose a coast

when my hands are stone?
Why a rifle when my blood is a field?
I carry these suitcases full of rain

because I can't take my country.
If it's a choice you want—I've never known
a world that wasn't worth dying for.

Zeina Hashem Beck

Ghazal: Back Home

for Syria, September 2015

Tonight a little boy couldn't walk on water or row back home.
The sea turned its old face away. Again, there was a *no, no,* back home.

Bahr is how we were taught to measure poetry,
bahr is how we've stopped trying to measure sorrow, back home.

"All that blue is the sea, and it gives life, gives life," says God to the boy
standing wet at heaven's gate—does he want to return, to go back
home?

My friend who hates cooking has made that eggplant dish,
says nothing was better than yogurt and garlic and tomato, back
home.

On the train tracks, a man shouts, "Hold me, hold me," to his wife,
bites her sleeve, as if he were trying to tow back home.

Thirteen-year-old Kinan with the big eyes says, "We don't want to
stay in Europe."
"Just stop the war," he repeats, as if praying, *Grow, grow back, home.*

Habibi, I never thought our children would write HELP US on
cardboard.
Let's try to remember how we met years ago, back home.

On our honeymoon we kissed by the sea, watched it
rock the lights, the fishing boats to and fro, back home.

Note: Bahr is Arabic for sea. Also, in Arabic poetry, *bahr* means meter.

Zeina Hashem Beck

Naming Things
for refugees, September 2015

Angels—
we saw them on the railway, the street,
covered with dust.
We licked our fingers and wrote
رحلنا
on their wings.

Wings—
my daughter left them on her bed,
cried when she remembered.
We found a dead seagull by the sea,
before we took the inflatable boat,
and I plucked a feather for her.
She smiles, but still asks
about our cat.

Cats—
all your life you've loved them and yet
believed they brought you bad luck. Every time
we adopt one, we lose a vase, a soul, and now,
a country. Let's sleep in that little alley
where the cats walk
on the edge of
~~refuge~~ refuse bins.

Country—
the trees will seem barren
will seem heavy with fruit
will make you cry, like onions.
Your eyes will be fine. Remember
the name your parents gave you
has plenty of shade. Rest in it.

Onions—
my kind of moon, the kind
you could cut through,
the kind you could eat. Not
that rubber globe in the sky,
its heart full of air.

The heart—
never learns
keeps coming back
to the same songs,
the same wars.

War—
hums, *I will make love*
to you in a bed of blood and faith,
will show you her lips,
hide her teeth, her money-scented
breath, the rust on her tongue, the children
underneath her fingernails.

Tongue—
they've burnt
Aeham's piano
on his birthday.
He has left Yarmouk for Germany.
Remember the vodka,
back when we were students,
drunk in your car? Our youth
is still in the back seat. The dust
was so beautiful; I watched it fall
all afternoon, in the sun.

The sun—
does not need us
is not a blanket
films us with its glare
do I look oh-so-cinematic

more dramatic in this light,
mr. le photographe?
Do my eyes my hands
tell a story?

Stories—
I try to tell my boys
we are backpacking through Europe.
My great grandmother, who had lost her mind
to old age, used to talk about a monster
in the trees. Chops people off and cooks them.
Like this, she'd say, moving her fingers as if
she were rolling a sandwich, and I'd become
afraid. And hungry.

Hunger—
the sea is a cemetery.
That fish you grilled last night,
did it laugh? Did it say, *I have been feeding
on your children*? It tasted good
with olive oil and lemon and garlic.
My mother always said everything
(even the dead) tastes good
with olive oil and lemon and garlic.

Mother—
land

mother—
tongue
mama
told a journalist
she'd go back to the war
if they allowed me into Germany.
*No problem, just take her,
let her pass*, she said,
as she combed my hair.

My hair—
or is that seaweed? Grass?

Grass—
your father's clothes
will smell of him, as if he'd just
stepped out of them and went
to lie down underneath the grass.
Leave them there. They will grow
too heavy in the rain.

The rain—
fuck
even the rain, this
funeral song.
It, too, will go out to sea
and bury us.

Bury—
when I die,
you will recognize me by my tattoo.
I got it when I was twenty-three,
it says, و ما أطال النوم عمراً
"Sleep has never lengthened a life,"
and that is why we are those who love
watching the night, we call it سهر
and Leila comes over
every night for whiskey, laughs
and repeats *Ya Allah! Ya Allah!*

God—
is sometimes a camera,
sometimes has a nom de guerre,
and mostly he's that old drum
beating at the heart of my mother
language, giving me the urge to dance,
or a broken hip.

My hips—
are heavy
are child-bearing
child-killing
are lover
do not fit those
train windows
these fences
this escape this

Ra7eel—
so much in my *3arabi* depends
on *ra7eel* on

3awda—
a5 ya baba
I have fallen in love
with Beckett, I stumble
on my Arabic inflections, confuse
subject and object,
but I have promised Al-Mutanabbi
I will come back.

Promise—
some people are kind, say
Bienvenu, Welcome, أهلا
here's some water, here's a toy,
a sandwich, here
away from slaughter and also
from my balconies, my bed, my books.
There is no space for me
to make love to you here.

Here—
Nina Simone sings
Got my liver, got my blood,
so here, despite the children sleeping
on the floor, and the tents, and the sea,

45

and much much more,
kiss me, for where else
do we carry home now, *habibi*,
if not on our lips?

Notes:

1. Some images in this poem refer to newspaper and TV reports on the refugee crisis.
2. رحلنا is Arabic for "We have left."
3. و ما أطال النوم عمراً is a line from *The Rubaiyat of Omar Al-Khayyam*, famously sung by Umm Kulthum.
4. The words *ra7eel, 3awda,* and *3arabi* are written in "Arabizi," and they are Arabic for "departure," "returning," and "Arabic." The word "a5" is an Arabic sigh sound. "Arabizi" comes from the combination of the words "Arabic" and "Englizi" (English); it uses numbers to represent sounds that are specifically Arabic, and has become well-known among Arabic speakers (especially online and in texting). I've chosen to write these words this way (instead of Arabic, as I've done earlier in the poem) because of what the persona is saying about departing from her mother language/land.

Rewa Zeinati

Villages Have Names Too

I.
Guns. Mcdonald's. Steak knives. Journalists. Truck wheels. Bullets.
Suicide. Army boots. Home.

>allahuakbarallahuakbarallahu
>akbarallahuakbarallahuakbara
>llahuakbarallahuakbarallahuak

Disappear into a thousand million pieces. How one thing becomes
another. Will you find it in your G-d to forgive me?

II.
My mother's mother was a storyteller who was constantly interrupted.
We weren't supposed to know about the land, the longing.

III.
How many faceless virgins await the hero who.

>Seventy two. Twenty seven. Eleven. Eighty five. As if it.

>The world's bestseller.

>What kind
>of

>>love
>>story

>>>hard
>>>cover
>>>binding

You're saying it all wrong.
~~Am I?~~

IV.

Memories lived on her tongue like language/ her accent/ a secret weighed down/ by the stones of leaving/ and when I pretended that I wasn't listening,

V.

Raise your voice and raise your gun. Find a land and occupy it forever and tell the journalist how much it hurts to be here. Have children and tell them they've belonged here all along, tell them, it's only fair.

Where did all the birds go?

VI.

My mother's father was a quiet man I never met. And when the bombs came I was told he wouldn't leave the village church until his prayers were complete.

VII.

And when I pretended that I wasn't listening, I occupied myself by gazing at her peacock blue slippers, frail and thin, like her aging ankles that carried her from border to border.

And I've never seen
And I've never seen
And I've never seen

VIII.

But I've seen how eyes can refuse forgetting.

IX.

Falling requires distance from a high point, requires gravity or the absence of a kind of science or a kind of love. Requires fiction. And heroes dressed in robes and hymns and precious stones. Penises chocked in their fists. Forgive me/ did I say that out loud? Are you listening now?

X.

~~Look away.~~
Watch
a grown man
rummage through
street garbage
looking for food
or clothes or
broken glass

Think: how did he get here? Think: Did he hide his daughters *in his eyes, his heart*, isn't this how we express love in our tongue?

Think: This could've been your father.

Think: This isn't about you. Think: Of course it is.

XI.

She swam and swam the long-winded cough of the old sea. Pushed
a vessel full of families and fear into the crooked mouth of shore.
Joined the Olympics and showed us how water, too, keeps us whole.

XII.

    Stay in between the hours of twelve and four p.m.
    The rest of the time pray
    The rest of the time cook something
    The rest of the time rest
    The rest of the time mourn the ocean its fleet of dead birds in migration

XIII.

Death is good here. A celebration. Hang the faces of men, as old as
children, who killed and got killed. Hang them along the winding
roads that lead up to the mountains and down to the rivers. Forget the
rosebushes lining the path. Forget the pine trees. Or every other kind
that grows here. Remember only the faces of these men. Hang them like
flags over wrought iron balconies, like clean laundry drying in the sun.

Dying in the sun.

XIV.

I can't tell whose children these are. The ones who sell water bottles and balloons and small plastic drums. A girl runs between the slow cars in traffic. A boy runs to the open windows. On my right, the sea glows.

Parents hurl their bodies into the water, fully clothed, fully clothed.

XV.

Shall I name them? Will it make sense then? Palestine. Iraq. Syria. Yemen. Libya. Shall I name the cities? Will you finally listen? Beirut. Gaza. Aleppo. Haifa. *Sakhnin.*

Villages have names too.

XVI.

And when she died it was Easter and I was nowhere to be found.

XVII.

Everyone is somewhere else. The city is a pension home for the elderly. No one lives here anymore. We wait to go back, to forget dying. The blackouts of a thousand-year-old city. Aircraft as proud as birds. Air, the fragility of lungs.

XVIII.

Believe it: Windows are the eyes of the soul. Tucked behind thick blinds and broken. We must be half terrible, half

terrible. How else do we explain all this?

XIV.

He shoots at the blue patches between the branches/ says he might find something for lunch/ something small and delectable/ to drop down on him like rain.

Or maybe I imagined it. How one thing becomes another. Where did all the birds go?

Sharif S. Elmusa

I Want My House to Stand

I see. The houses are rubble,
twisted bars, stunned ghosts.
This is my shelter.
Many sleep and wake under the same roof.
Meals and stories from the same containers.
I hear. I lost my wife.
My daughter ran toward me:
Dad, I'm not afraid.
My son sits in the corner:
I don't like my mom,
she doesn't want to come back.
I lost nine members of my family.
Nine chairs are left empty.
I hear. I see. Sorrow mingles with the bread,
dust with the cold tea.
Sorrow piles up. Piles up:
The severed limbs of many loves,
the kids who will remain on holiday.
Time is slow, time flows into an icebox.
I hear. Why do they do this to us? Why?
A sport? To make us succumb?
I hear. The good helpers are unable to comfort.
The shelter does not shelter.
I want my house to stand.
I want the walls back
To weep alone
To hang pictures.

Ibtisam Barakat

My People's Story

We once lived rooted
Like the ancient olive trees.
Now we're birds
Nesting on songs
About homes we miss.
Storms and distances,
Decide our address.

Adele Ne Jame

A Chouf Lament

celebrate your land's spring
and set yourself a flame like its flowers
after M. Darwish

You wonder what will you do without
the cedars—the winding road up the mountain,
even the vegetable stand on the side of it

with the young boy piling okra and
green beans into his baskets to sell
there. His whole Chouf life

ahead of him—at least you'd like to think.
What will you do without the almond tree
and the mulberry in the March sun—.

And the mountain wind
shaking everything here alive.
The red earth, red clouds moving

over the village terraced
into the side of mountain. The sun—
insatiable. The hoopoe that flutters

her way up through the red clouds
to the snowy cedars. The blasted roses
in the rock gardens that are gathered by

villagers and distilled into perfumed
water to wash the bodies of the dead.
This is what you find in the high places:

the flourish of spring and the violence that
hangs in the red air.
The windblown cedars not far above

the abandoned stone houses,
Arabic script on a rotting window sill.
Homage to the ones marched into a snowy field,

their names inscribed on the wall in
St Michel's—where William rang the bells
beautifully one morning

so that we might forget
for a moment how, like the fields of

the wild red anemone, we are waving
our songs in the air before night falls.

Note: The Chouf refers to a high area of villages in Mount Lebanon, where one of the two last stands of the cedars of Lebanon referred to as" the Cedars of the Lord" remain at about 6,000 feet.

Nathalie Handal

Beit

I dream of a house where the ghosts are quiet
where their shape is like a sound in black,
well-defined and formless,
where I will invite everyone I know
and those I haven't met yet—
Will they come?
I will tell them to take a branch
from a tree and sit around the table—
in each leaf, an ancient pattern
from the Canaanites or the Greeks—
Strange are the lights that insist
on holding the walls together
but they do—don't they?
Will they come?
Will they move silently
in all directions of one room
and tell me the only story I want to hear—
that of a house in a country intact
with a grotto that gives hope
all the shapes of the universe?

Jehan Bseiso

After Aleppo

After Aleppo

I learned to read early.
But the truth is, sometimes I wish the letters remained funny
drawings for longer, before the uninvited tyranny of words, and
before other tongues found home in my big mouth.

I don't mean it literally.

One day, we will go back to Aleppo you said.

You don't mean it literally.

Habeebi four years ago we shouted for change, and now we are
citizens of border towns.
We go from Turkey, to Lebanon, to Egypt, but we don't find Aleppo.
We have food vouchers, and, assistance criteria, and, intermittent
empathy.

I don't write any more poetry.

The boat is sinking,
literally,
but I don't want to leave this room.
It smells like jasmine and you taste like freedom

TO FIT INTO OUR
BACKPACKS

Sanaa Shuaibi

I will look for myself and search for it
I will find it buried under the wreckage and the
crowds
I will find it in-between confusion and wishing
Between pain and wounds
I will bury my feelings in my heart
And collect my memories and leave
I will get up and triumph and be the strongest
With my experience, my choice and my decision
I will look for love, honesty and hope
I will be the master of myself and my thoughts
I will not kneel, I will not surrender
And will never beg as a slave.

Sanaa Shuaibi

Oh sea, don't cry and make us cry—
Swallow your tears, tears hurt us...
When will you know that the waves are our
homeland...
Because no country has land to harbor us...
Oh sea, don't cry for people...
Who made rocks cry but not the Sultans...
All countries are shut in front of the guests' faces...
Only the sky I see welcoming us...

Lena Khalaf Tuffaha

Fragment

There's nothing living here,
Only sea shells warped to the shapes
of their exiled residents,
trinkets from the kingdom of childhood.
The forecast calls for white phosphorus
with occasional sun breaks
barrel bombs in the afternoon,
and in the evening
checkpoints and falling temperatures.
We reach for what is useful,
a skin to wear between weather
patterns, a flame resistant faith,
hope enough
to fit into our backpacks

Angela Farmer

Stories from the Sea

Eftalou, Lesvos

Each time I go swimming
in the cold waters

there are more stories to drag
heavy and sodden up onto the land.

I wonder about each piece
who travelled in it

the fears and the prayers
the loved ones they clung to

and did they survive,
shout with joy as they neared safe shores?

where are they now
or did they too sink into the deep cold sea?

I say a prayer as I pull up a baby's vest,
a tangled sweater

and today a flowered bra,
two socks and a woman's lined jacket.

The clothes will dry
and be gathered up to recycle or burn...

Too many stories,
so many lives.

Lisa Suhair Majaj

Exile, Edge

We walked uphill on a razor-edge.
We walked without knowing
where we were going or if we would arrive.

Each of us carried something.
A bundle, a bag, a sack of broken dreams,
a key tucked close to the heart,

the future slung across our backs.
We walked out of our lives along a blade
of hope. We walked into the blue,

a chasm yawning on either side.
We had been told there was refuge ahead,
but the horizon was empty.

The path was slippery, red-streaked.
We hardly noticed. There would be time later
for the staunching of wounds,

for grieving what could not be healed.
We walked through rain and sun,
through dark and light: the past inside of us,

the present teetering on the abyss.
Balancing is a trick, we told the children.
Don't look up, don't look down, don't let your gaze waver.

But our feet are bleeding, they protested.
Yes, we replied. Hoist your bundle,
look straight ahead, walk.

after the artwork Syrian Exile, *by Moustafa Jacoub*
in memory of Andreas Anelxandrou, who also walked a blade of hope

Fatma Al Hassan

Wound of the Homeland

How can I be happy and our wound is bleeding and
ulcerating
How can I be happy and my people are emigrating
under the bombing
Oh my country, my love, don't cry
for the thrones of injustice are swinging
Oh my country's soil, tell the story of who sacrificed
and who succeeded
But the separation from our beloved is harder and
harsher
The blood around me is a sea and the slavery is
swimming inside
Soon a boat will be drawn that killed and terrorized
Soon our flag will rise, soon my people will win
The masks of the world have fallen, what a black
and ugly face it has
It wants a national division; it wants a nation that
is teetering
It wants a civil war; we don't agree and shall not
allow
The truth is revealed from falsehood and the game
on us will not be won
And the people swore to sacrifice their blood
to Damascus and conquer
Because unity is necessary to succeed.

Sharif S. Elmusa

An Update of Our Fall

The hair delicate
The waves combed it
As if composing lines
Lamenting the deed
The mouth is turned away
From the salt and sand
The ear a pearl's shell
The murmurs of the tale still wet
To us he shows
Not his bright face
But his back
At us he looks
Not with the keen eyes
But with the soles of the sandals
A picture of parts
An update of our fall
The tiny palm of his hand
Cupped
Mute petals
Beyond time
Beyond border

Sanaa Shuaibi

Little Dreams

Birds and small boat
Where are you traveling, where are you migrating
To
Isn't there any shore or anchorage
Or do we stay like this in exile
I have no address and no homeland anymore
To which country do I belong.

Sanaa Shuaibi

Long night?
Excuse me!
Your moon has become pale and its joy has
disappeared
The dark clouds are suffocating it like thorns
They stole its light and smile and made it sad
They deprived its passions away and left it dead
Without love...without a feeling
Tenderness, night, to whom is in love

THE FACTS ARE FACES

Gbenga Adesina

What She Says

Hauwa, 13, in the camp on discovering she was carrying the child of one of her abductors

I touch my belly
And say to him die
Wither, river out, do not
Become a thing.

I say to him
Stay as night. You are night.
No dawn, no dawn.
Please die.

Golan Haji

Disappearances

To My Youngest Sister

Sister, I am you. Your shoes are little arks for frightened animals,
they are me looking at you.
No dog barked when the two small strangers came to the blind
orchard, where their grandfather's curse flapped overhead like the
clatter of his shrine's door.
You play the role of the prey, you are dying in a place I know like the
palm of my hand, and I cry, tormented, in a locked room.
The ceiling fan questions your neck, your long inscrutable silence,
my own silence that unlooses the din of your heart, fear because
everything is frightening now, the intruders are behind you.
Stretched out like an invalid under the covers, you lose yourself in
the clouds, with the tears I begged you to hold back.
Now my body is the sole site of my suffering, the kiss that waited so
long to arrive on your cheek found it cold as a stone in the rain.

To Raed Naqshabandi

What you were given to bear was heavier than you'd have thought.
Deir az-Zour, that green knife-slash in the sand, that gathered up
the bus of the dead, your near and dear whom I didn't know, my
wounded friends. We kept crossing the river in both directions, and
we saw other buses, the cafés on the two riverbanks, the foreigners'
cemetery behind the bus station and the swimmers' candles in the
deep water. We heard songs as we crossed that were not merely the
night's longing. I asked you: Will your little Alhamra cigarettes help
you out more than God? Will you beat him at chess tomorrow, and
set him a forfeit, saying "Read what I wrote backwards in this old
notebook!" He would need a mirror deeper than blood to read your
sorrow there, and your silence.

To Akkad Nizam ad-Din

They speak to you of roofs, but what about the depths?
Your own eyes' light will be enough for you to leave by the tunnel drawn on the wall.
Enter it without looking back. That metallic noise in the dusk is only the rust on the locks and the door hinges.
You will cut into the cypress fruit to smell it, and you'll hum a tune as beautiful as you are.
Your heart is your skiff, and your dream will bring you back from beneath the earth
On the other side, there is a song I never listened to with you.
And the schoolbooks you blasted apart with a rifle at the gun club, because you venerate nothing.

To Mohammed Samy al-Kayyâl

I didn't know you yet that long-ago winter, your coat drenched from the drizzle and your beard silky as the breath of the grass. In the cinema lobby, I said to my friend "That fellow there looks like Chesterton!" Like silent strangers, we watched "The Seventh Seal," and Death in Bergman's film was a clown who made you laugh. During your illness, you thought of an-Niffari, of historians, of children's drawings: what the child said who had drawn an animal with his fingers so his drawing-paper was blank. "The dinosaurs aren't extinct, but now they're transparent."
From house to house, from continent to continent, from the café al-Kamal to the Saruja square, behind all the books, there was the tenderness of your shadow and friends' hands nostalgic for the warmth of yours.

To Ruwa Riché

What's the matter with you?
Have pity on me, don't ask me any questions!
What are you doing these days?
I write letters to the disappeared, and I hide. The light in the streets is painful, and the curtains are ugly.

Where do you sleep?
My eyes are embalmed in front of a computer screen, and my heart
flutters like the little orphans holding scales on the sidewalks.
What are you doing now?
I transform the heat that I silenced into words. I think of my friends'
pain, and of mothers' hands. I am learning how to live.
Did the fist open up to welcome you?
Not at all! It turned into a slap. Now my neck is a thick sprained
cable.
What did you say?
I am not sensitive. I'm sick. My tongue is a saw and my words a torn
net. Every voice bears a bit of the death of its owner.
How would you like to sleep?
Deeply, like someone who has slain fear with one cry, once and for
all.
What do you dream about?
I don't remember my dreams, but I create them.
Are you alone?
Like you, like all of us.
Are you afraid?
Afraid for life, that drips into the abyss, or that grants us what we're
afraid to lose.
What is hardest in every chaos?
Confronting those who are like us.
Have you traveled?
I carry a door I can't see. When someone knocks, it wakes me, even
if I lay down to sleep out in the open. There is always a slight delay.
Fear is no emotion, it's reality. And I'm in the same place wherever I
am, because I'm incapable of forgetting.
Where are you headed?
When I started out, I found myself at the end of the road, and my
steps took flight.

Translated from Arabic by Marilyn Hacker

Ahmad Almallah

States of Being in Holy Land

Regions of sorrow, doleful shades, where peace
And rest can never dwell, hope never comes
—John Milton, *Paradise Lost*

I

The leaves are facts, the facts are faces
in the dark, their branches do not leave signs
of time and wonder. These ripe faces
fading by the count of hours upon hours.
These shadows upon which, day after day,
I trip, I stumble, they've taken every
thing I say, every sound I make, away!

It has all been exhausted, it's almost
gone, summer! And once upon these longings,
Oh once upon this time and that, I thought,
this house, these walls, can keep the world away.

The streets do not tire of their harsh steps,
and when they are empty, they are flowing.
No night, no morning brightness can save them.

II

I get up, I wash my face beginning
with indifference, I take a step, two
I take one back, and from step to step, I
pause behind the door. The hand cannot take
this handle: home, beginning of love, desire,
land of olive branches and white doves:
I close my eyes to your misery, I wish.

III

I've been through all of this, I know.
The night has come with no silence.
The sound of fireworks in lonely
darkness. I remain, sleepless, still.

Morning comes so suddenly,
the call to prayer, the time now
is now the time, to get up, leave,
pause at the door, and place the hand.

We will go to the mosque again,
to the prayer of the Eid, we walk
the empty streets, the ones flowing
with morning sunshine and litter.

We've been through all of this, we know
the way to greet uncles and aunts,
the time to stop at each check point,
as our occupiers hand over life.

IV

"What matters where, if I be still the same,"
this home is where, I long to part with me.

Mohja Kahf

Oncologist

Oncologist
Smoker, despite her training
Transfusing, scowling, transecting
Assad army assaults ad-hoc hospital
Salvaging, trekking, scavenging
Brutalized, caged
Survivor

Hajer Almosleh

140

I spend the day looking at corpses
crouched against each other
the bomb
has found the baby's soft spot
aimed with precision
and fell
ripping through the mother's hands
still cradling the baby's head
I try to reconstruct the face
imagine the color of the swaddle
draw the shape of the eyes
the name
this Wednesday of ashes

Marilyn Hacker

Nieces and Nephews

In July, when Tsahal was bombing Gaza
and we marched, and there were flags and brawls
Lamis waited for me on the corner, smiling
in a lime-green sleeveless dress, not her daily jeans.
There were three cop cars parked in front of my building
and Lamis shouted giddily in Arabic
"She's the terrorist, here!" I pinched her,
shushed her, laughing "Half those cops are Arabs!"
We went to a café, drank wine. She told me
her niece had finally been freed from prison
in Damascus. She lit up her cell phone
to show me the 19-year-old girl's photo.
The second of her older sister's children.
Naima's Ismaël on the Corniche, sunlit
in a rust corduroy jacket, white shirt open
at the neck, smiles next to his aunt in paisley
hijab and movie-star dark glasses.
Wind scuds the waves beyond. Out of Mosul
for the first time in his life, she, out of danger
for the first time in six months. The last
check-point, the last baksheesh, the abaya
shoved into a suitcase. A walk on Sunday,
a future open as the wine-dark sea.
I drank wine in the same café with Rasha
last week, at midnight, talking about meters—
blank verse, alexandrines and al-mursal—
though she was keen to go outside and smoke
in the insidious slant winter rain.
"Have you heard from Lamis? I haven't seen her
in a month, she didn't answer an e-mail."
"Her nephew," said Rasha, "died in prison
under torture." The first of those five children.
I'll meet Ismaël in Beirut with Naima.
In Beirut, no one arrests the daughters

or the nephews of the neighbors these days,
so she can bitch and moan about the neighbors
and how her students can't translate as-Sayyab
"Nothing but Iraq..." The rain is falling
on all the suburbs where it lives in exile
and Lamis isn't answering the phone.

Marisa Frasca

Under the Sky of Lampedusa

Tell me little one
what name your precious mother chose to give you
was it gift
was it flower

Tell me little one
when your breasts began to bud
did your brother frown
stand firm with stick in hand to scare your suitors

Did you walk holding your father's arm

Did he secretly smile when young men called you beautiful

For elder faces of your desert village
were you breath of air

maybe high tower when you climbed the boat of hope
never making that last 1/2 mile of desperate crossing

Tell me little one
what name
to give these men in face masks
carrying the bloodless body on a stretcher

what name
to search and rescue
tagging the bloated blue-black ankle
#99

Nora M. Barghati

Exodus

In herds
of hundreds and thousands
they move
in a raw stampede.
Men dragging their women
women dragging their flesh and bone
—their own—
and their own
dragging empty bellies
and empty words.
Bare feet that bleed
along the way
leave a trace
that extends like the hand of God
clutching onto what once was
and is no more.
With dry eyes
and throats that are sore
they watch the vultures soar
around the fallen
and the ill
and wonder
when
will I be next?
Trampling on
the rotting corpse
of humanity
they hurry
they rush
to fit into our modern day
Noah's Ark.

Sara Saleh

Aylan

your shadow permanently refracts on the back of my retina
i can't see sunbathers by the beach
without your 3-year-old face
a flood of a million more
like you
desperate enough to leave their homelands
their loved ones, their language and their lineage
to find new family to give love back to the parts
of themselves they've forgotten
to search for safety and the welcomes
waiting in the curves of our lips
our arms once a roadmap,
our mouths a single tent
our teeth open borders
for all those that came before

but you...
did you know that morning when you woke up,
tomorrow on the edge of your promises
that you would lose your child to the breaking of the waves?

did you smell like arguments and first loves?
did you haemorrhage out your memories,
hold him the way branches hold each other
in light spilled from sacred sunset
did you silence the question marks in their eye-lids
fight wars til you were all martyred?
did the belly of the seabed split right through you?

you were on your way to life, and we lost you
somewhere between
turn back the boats and we've conveniently misplaced our humanity

did you forget the neighbors built razor fences with
the fire in your brother's bones, now you float
across our feeds, our insta empathy not as deep
as the shallow waters that
whispered you out like secrets

did you run from your village that day,
knowing that the ocean is easier to swallow than staying?
that soon we'd scroll past your story in statues, memes
and in between trending tweets with no emoji for dignity
that we'd see and oversee and unsee
your slumber at sea, festishize your
image for a "like"

did you watch the world end in the blue of your skin?
your face in the sand a slogan stuck in our throats, a refugee crisis
in the dark folds of your hair, your lifeless limbs spread across
this city like a prayer rug

but their tongues can't carry the brownness
of your name the way
your mother used to
the way the tide has become
fluent in bodies
one after the other
after the other,
after the other.

did you know
you'd have to die
so we would let you in?

Adele Ne Jame

Interlude

Fairuz sings, her smooth almond-honey voice
sweeping all of Beiteddine—
give me just five minutes—under these mountain stars
and the whistling crowd is carried away—
bodies swaying to the jazz piano,
in the dazzling blue light.
How they love her, village girl turned diva
draped in turquoise and pearls.
Thousands wave their arms overhead for
the smoldering voice they call the desert wind.
The wind that shakes the date palms
Heavy with fruit—the sea wind over
the bombed out districts of Beirut
and in the Chouf, over the shrapnel-studded
cedars of the Lord. Over the blasted road to Damascus
where in the Christ light, Saul became Paul,
believer in signs and dreams.
The war ravaged. What the exhausted call
the dark years—one militia against another
raining down RPGs in the streets.
Or death squads in the mountains,
marching villagers into fields of wild
dandelions and snow—.
They have a saying here: it's quiet until it's not.
So during an interlude like this, we walk
the Corniche, fill our sacks with
Arabic coffee and oranges for breakfast.

And the ether of a warm summer night,
when the orchestra strikes up an old tune
and Fairuz turns to us—
with her shivering call—*ra'eeni* and again,
ra'eeni: care for me—we are transported—
delirious and clapping with her, as if
out there in heaven or on earth
somewhere, someone might really hear.

Merna Ann Hecht

Tell Me

Tell me about a pair of turquoise espadrilles
how they enclosed small, sun-brown feet
of a little girl who walked
through the Baghdad market
holding her uncle's hand.

Tell me, did she skip rope,
read beneath a generous tree,
legs crossed at the ankle,
her turquoise shoes
pointing up toward a matching sky?

Tell me of her daydreams,
of a still afternoon when dust motes danced
around her, how she splashed cool water on her face,
and ate one sweet date brought in from the country.

Can you show me her eyes,
bright moons in desert sky,
can you hear her trusting blue-clothed feet running
to pour mint tea when aunties came to call,
when slips of sun laughed on tiles and stories
ripened in common rhyme of time-worn moments?

Tell me
why her shoes stand empty.
Show me one reason for her death
all that is left,
an empty innocence,
filling small turquoise shoes.

Can you tell me,
who will be left,
who can speak her name
again
and again?

Jose A. Alcantara

Countertop

I run my hand along the surface
and feel the smoothness of volcanic glass.

The granite comes all the way from India,
but when I look closely, I see nebulae.

I see galaxies. I see little black suns
orbited by little black planets,

and on the planets, deep black holes
dug by broken black bodies.

And I see the black bodies heaving black stones,
and the stone burnished in black blood,

and buffed by black bone,
to the smoothness of volcanic glass.

And on the counter I lay bread, apples and cheese,
green olives, and those little swords we use

to stab the olives, bringing them to our mouths
without dirtying our hands.

Hayan Charara

On the Death of Other People's Children

Their deaths astonish
even the trees

but in no time we live again
the joys
they lost
and never knew.

Someone must
tell their mothers and fathers
to eat, drink, sleep,
to sing and dance.

And someone else
must tell them
not to.

Bronwen Griffiths

Sailing to Eternity

Who lies here at the bottom of the sea,
lost but not forgotten?
The ties of seaweed knotting her hair
as she clasps the child in her arms
for all eternity.
What country did she flee
for this over-crowded, listing, pirate-boat?
What exile has forced her to walk the plank
and place her weary feet upon the leaking wooden boards
with only her child and hope for company?
Slippery, drowned hope
No rope or raft to hold her
No lifeboat, no warm hand
No embrace but her child and the empty sea

Abu Bakr Khaal

African Titanics

Here, in the desert,
the sand refuses
to conceal the remains
of the migrant
forever.

Here, in the desert,
the sand lets
the hair
which splits
from the scalp
of the migrant
grow nearby.

Here, the all-knowing dunes
depict the Eritrean migrant
drugged
and tied with ropes.
While the heedless soul
is passed out,
the physician's hands sneak in
to plunder the mine.

He strips the kidneys
as the drops of blood
scream
like tears
bemoaning the swindled body.
He scrutinizes the lobes of the lung
and settles for
the left lobe.

Corneas are extracted
like oyster

from a shell.
Then the corpus is dumped
tied
and choked.

But, the eye of the all-knowing dunes
tells the passers-by
about restless bones
underneath the sand
and about hair
shooting up like grass
and a skull that rests
like a dove
on the dust
of the corpus.

Translated from Arabic by Mootacem Bellah Mhiri

Khaled Mattawa

Psalm for the Balkan Route
At peace in the palm: embers,
perfumes, the scents of Abyssinia
and Mecca haunt the brain.

You remember weddings and feasts.
Hail pocked the copper dust, and you,
opened-mouthed, gazed at the world.

Years have passed since that since.
How does the body know how to pin
so much of itself in words?

Psalm for Arrival
When we find the sounds
for words we need, their death
rattle begins to echo in our throats.

Memory creeps up on old sentiments,
finds them lurking like blind fish
in the twilight of our blood.

Dead and living on—ancient prophesies
or frozen microbes—something we disavow
continues to feed on us.

Psalm for the Medic
The road to paradise, an avalanche
                of blood, swerved away
        from them.

They hear a breath,
                launch their sirens
        through piled towers blinding dust,

shovel to concrete muffled moans—
O eyes heed—
bodies snapped into silence—

Blow, mouth, into beaten lungs!
Even God had to light the clay
with his cold breath—

Hand, slap the new tender flesh—
Fingers, retrieve a cry
from the throbbing umbilical cord

Psalm for the Deportee
Between privilege and pity
a paradise of tolerable solitude,
a checkpoint at a hope that slides.

The traveler is cornered at last:
voice encased in thirst, his body
is midnight, past spirit and cup.

Eman Abdelhadi
The Lost

to the ones we lost
the ones who faded on the horizon of memory
and the ones severed into phantom limbs
and the ones who walked over the edge of yesterday
and the ones threaded between our breaths
to the ones who visit only in dreams
to the ones who live beneath the skin
you're still here; goodbye.

IS HOME MY GHOST?

Sholeh Wolpé

The World Grows Blackthorn Walls

Tall, stiff and spiny.
Try to make it to the other side
and risk savage thorns.

We who left home in our teens,
children who crossed boundaries and were torn
by its thousand serrated tongues,
                            who have we become?

We who bear scars that bloom and bloom
beneath healed skins,
                        where are we going?

I ask myself:
                    is home my ghost?

Does it wear my underwear
folded neatly in the antique chest
of drawers I bought twenty years ago?
Or nest inside my blouse that hangs
from a metal hanger I've been meaning to discard?
Is it lost between the lines of books
shelved alphabetical in a language
I was not born to? Or here on the lip
of this chipped cup left behind
by a lover long gone?

Why do they call us *alien*,
as if we come from other planets?

I carry seeds in my mouth, plant
turmeric, cardamom, and tiny
aromatic cucumbers in this garden,
water them with rain I wring

from my grandmother's songs.
They will grow, I know, against
these blackthorn walls. They are magic.

They can push through anything,
                                        Uncut.

I left home at thirteen.
I hadn't lived enough to know how
not to love.
Home was the Caspian Sea, the busy bazaars,
the aroma of kebab and rice, friday
lunches, picnics by mountain streams.
                        I never meant to stay away.

But they said come back
                        and you will die.

Exile is a suitcase full of meanings. I fill up
a hundred notebooks with scribbles.
And when I am done I throw them into fire
and begin to write again; this time
tattooing the words on my forehead.
This time, writing only not to forget.

Complacency is communicable
like the common cold.
I swim upstream to lay my purple eggs.

Spirits urge and spirits go,
But I write postcards only to the future.
What is a transplanted tree
But a *time being*
Who has adapted to adoption?

They say draw sustenance from this land,
but look how my fruits hang in spirals
and smell of old notebooks and lace.

Perhaps it's only in exile that spirits arrive.
They weep and wail at the door of the temple
where I sit at the edge of an abyss.
But even this is an illusion.

Saad Abdullah

Kiss the Jasmine

Allow me to kiss the jasmine
Let me stand on the threshold of your garden
Let me smell what I long for
Amongst the grains of sand on your beach.

Don't kill the lovestruck stars
Don't tell the sun and the moon to be silent
Let them speak.

Oh you, traveler through ages
Take from my hand the key to my house,
Take my name, take the jasmine.

Because I am now homeless
Between my past and your future
Between the sea, the camp, the harbor.

Why do you use my name but abuse my being?
I curse you in the name of god.
Why do you punish my mind and my spirit?
I curse you in the name of god.

What makes you think your blood
is different from my blood?
What repels you about my name—"refugee"
You who gave me this name?

Translated from Arabic with Zoe Holman.

Sara Abou Rashed

Welcome to America

Bring us your oppressed, your exhausted bodies,
your hungry, unheard crowds and we shall set them free

"I'd like to welcome you to the one and only,
the greatest America." Says the lady
in the white shirt behind a desk.
"Now honey, please fill out all these papers,
and don't forget to send us your story,
why you came here, your hopes and expectations.
We wish you a happy life."
...
16 springs I've witnessed, not one
was blooming, there,
behind the shores of the Mediterranean,
everything is a martyr, there—
we don't dare live lest we die,
even roses grow stripped of colors.

Though, the scarred walls there memorize
our names, though the tarred roads
there know our stories.

But here,
to every ally, to every town,
I must introduce myself:
No, no, I am sorry, I am not who
you think I am.
No, I am not who they say I am.

See,
I am as much of a human as you are;
I brush my teeth, I sleep, I cry when hurt and bleed when injured,
I walk the land you walk, I breathe
the same air you breathe, your American dream
is my dream, I am afraid of what you're afraid of.

Please, don't stop me on streets to ask what Jihad is,
don't mistake me for one of them, don't stare at me like an alien,
like a one-eyed, four-legged, green monster of your nightmares.

I am a woman of faith,
a citizen not a suspect.
I carry a breaking heart within, I hold mics not guns—
my story refuses to be told in bullets and word limits.

And no, I don't celebrate the death of children,
I don't wish to destroy homes and churches.

Trust me, I know what loss smells like:
the way fear and revolution play tug of war
on doorsteps, uproot loved ones from
framed pictures on walls, steal a father
from the dinner table—I can only hope
mine hears me now.

I know what loss smells like from a mile far, the way friends
tell you they saw your house tear asunder
like it was never there:
the old gate, the dolls, grandma's garden and every
dream we've built on the roof with hands too small
to plant hatred.

Still, some fear me, they call me names, they try to break
me, to wreck me, to ricochet me, but
my spine will keep mountains standing,
my knees will only ever kneel to my Lord:

Lord, make us whole again, all of us, make us human again,
forgive us for we have sinned, and Lord,
guide them to see me for who I am, because
I, too yearn for peace, because I drop poems, not bombs.

Zoe Holman

All Necessary Measures

London, August 30, 2013 (House of Commons votes against air strikes on Syria)

Despite the health warnings,
they couldn't say what happened at the school.
There were things smeared, a burning substance
the walking dead. A smell
faintly acrid across the airwaves
of the AM broadcast. But anyhow

that mess was distant now.
The leaden cloud had passed, unbreached. Its cool
horrors would make deluge
for others' heads, leave the small
ecstasy of partisanship below, undisturbed—
hawkish hearts to bleed and bleeding hearts to mend
to commend, pat flagellated backs. *A good innings.*

A quick sound bite for the 6 o'clock and then
a pint on the deck at Bellamy's
close allies and friends, flanked
by all our flaxen war-tested spires.
There are bicycles and banners, and
paella scalding copper-pots on the Southbank.
It is the last Friday of summer and all that fire—
the nightmare—is somebody else's.

Omar Alsayyed

Misplaced Home

The paint faded,
The ghosts moved away,
And no one's left to listen to me sing.

If these walls could speak,
They'd tell stories of the night
Our memories buried themselves in the backyard.

I try serenading the silences
With all the lullabies my mother has written,
But the echoes are too loud for me to hear myself play.

Every undusted patch
Of light steeps in dusk blues,
In rooms where air is denser than honey.

The silver tarnished,
The reflections withdrew,
And no one's left to look back into my eyes.

Fouad Mohammed Fouad

The Corridor

The wolf in the corridor
A soul at loose ends
In the space adjacent the morgue
Where antiseptics are less useful
And those passing by
Only pass with their heads bent.

Let the gauze bandages unroll in the waiting room
And follow the drop of blood

The patients are sick with cruelty
An acrid grease-stain on the bed

The wolf in the corridor
His shadow wounds the little girl
And the grandmother

Don't roll up your stained shirt beneath your head
Don't ask why the woman behind the door is weeping

The wolf in the corridor

Stop the music
He is dying

Translated from the Arabic by Marilyn Hacker

Mohja Kahf

Who by Fire (Syria, 2017)

after Leonard

Whose whole family, whose half family
bombed in the basement, died in revolution time
Who fled the country on foot through the woods
Who by Mediterranean, who subterranean
Who went bankrupt, who embezzled orphans' funds
Who still eats out at Damascus restaurants

Who by sarin gas, who by militia knife
Who with father killed sold tea in the street
Who fell from sniper fire, who fell in first love
Who from the torture tire, broken in leg and mind
Who became a child soldier, who became a child bride
Who lost six years of school, who finished her Ph.D.,

just to regain some sense of normalcy
Who after *shabiha* rape took her own life
Who came out queer to claim a new life
Who is living on revolution time
Who isn't living on revolution time
And who shall I say is dying

Becky Thompson

Squatters' Rights

LGBTQI Refugee Gala, Athens, 2017

Squatting in an abandoned building in Exarchia Square, they
Up the ante of who can shimmy their hips faster
As the gay chef from Syria orchestrates a four course dinner
That will stretch to feed fifty. The Afghan family who lives upstairs wanders in,
Their toddler dancing with a transgender woman with
Effervescent eyes who tells us, "my sisters and I risked the raft,
Ravages of bombs now behind us, a hole in the boat the
Size of my fist, which we filled with singing until we were
Rescued." *Paris is Burning* travels to Athens on a dinghy,
Inclusion the mantra folded into tabouli. Salt translates into Arabic and Urdu,
Gracious a verb everyone is granted, as the bass from the sound system
Hijacks old fear. Temporary becomes an excuse for let's party, community
Traveling with tattoos and silk scarves. The toddler sleeps in a crook of an arm as
Silence equals death transforms into eyes from this storm.

Ibtisam Barakat

A Song for Alef

Alef the letter
Is a refugee.
From paper
To paper
He knows
No home.

Alef the letter,
He is the shape
Of a key
To the postal box
Of memory.

Alef the letter
Sits in the front
Of the bus
Of alphabets
To see.
He sees war,
He looks above it.
He sees war,
He looks below it.
And beyond it
To see peace.

Alef knows
That a thread
Of a story
Stitches together
A wound.

Alef the letter
He's the shape
Of hope.

Like me,
A refugee.

For me,
My refuge.

Sholeh Wolpé

The Outsider

I know what it's like to be an outsider, a *kharejee.*

I know how English sounds
when every word is only music.

I know how it feels not
to be an American, an English, a French.
Call them
        —Amrikayee, Ingleesee, Faransavi,
see them
        see me as alien, immigrant, *Iranee.*

But I've been here so long
they may call me American,
        with an American husband
        and American children...

But mark this—I do not belong anywhere.
I have an accent in every language I speak.

Sinan Antoon

Afterwords

My father's warm palms shielded my ears. I could hear his blood racing in his veins. As if being chased by the bombs falling outside. My mother's lips fluttered like a terrified butterfly. She was talking to God and asking him to protect us. That's what she did the last war. And he listened. Her arms were clasped around my two sisters. Maybe God could not hear her this time. The bombing was so loud. After our house in Jabalya was destroyed we hid in the UNRWA school. But the bombs followed us there too...

and found us.

***

Mother and father lied
We didn't stay together
I walked alone for hours

They lied
There are no angels
Just people walking
Many of them children

The teacher lied too
My wounds didn't become anemones
like that poem we learned in school says

***

Sidu didn't lie
He was there
Just as he'd promised me
before he died
He is here
I found him
Leaning on his cane
Thinking of Jaffa

When he saw me
He spread his arms wide
Like an eagle
A tired eagle with a cane
We hugged
He kissed my eyes

    ***

- Are we going back to Jaffa, *sidu*?
- We can't
- Why?
- We are dead
- So are we in heaven, *sidu*?
- We are in Palestine *habibi*
and Palestine is heaven

...

and hell
- What will we do now?
- We will wait
- Wait for what?
- For the others

...

to return

sidu: grandfather
habibi: my love

About the Editors:

Jehan Bseiso is a Palestinian poet, researcher, and aid worker. Her poetry has been published in *Warscapes, The Funambulist, The Electronic Intifada*, and *Mada Masr,* among others. Her co-authored book *I Remember My Name* (2016) is the creative category winner of the Palestine Book Awards. She is also working on a collection of poems, *Conversations Continued*, a compilation of real, misheard, and misremembered conversations. Jehan has been working with Médecins sans Frontières/Doctors Without Borders since 2008.

Becky Thompson, Ph.D., scholar, yogi, professor, and poet, is the author of multiple books, most recently, *Teaching with Tenderness* and *Zero is the Whole I Fall into at Night,* which received the Creative Justice Poetry Prize. Becky's writing and activism have been recognized with honors from the Rockefeller Foundation, the National Endowment for the Humanities, the Ford Foundation, and the Gustavus Myers Award for Outstanding Books on Human Rights. She has taught at China Women's University, Duke University, the University of Colorado, and Wesleyan University and is currently Professor of Sociology at Simmons University in the US. Since 2015, Becky has been traveling to Greece, meeting rafts, walking with refugees, assisting people seeking asylum, documenting human rights violations, and teaching poetry workshops. She leads yoga, creative writing, and social justice workshops in China, Thailand, and the US. For more about her work please visit: http://beckythompsonyoga.com.

About the Contributors

Eman Abdelhadi, born to an Egyptian mother and Palestinian father, is a queer activist, academic, writer, and poet. She is pursuing a doctorate in sociology at New York University.

Saad Abdullah is a 24-year-old poet from Aleppo, Syria. He studied archaeology and pharmacy before departing for Turkey in 2016. He lives in Athens and considers his sole weapon to be his pen, tongue, mind, and spiritual insight.

Gbenga Adesina, a young Nigerian poet, is a Starworks Poetry Fellow at New York University, where he teaches undergraduate creative writing. His work has been published in the *New York Times*, *Prairie Schooner,* and elsewhere.

Jose A. Alcantara has worked as a bookseller, mailman, fisherman, baker, photographer, salesman, and math teacher. He lives in Colorado and has poems published widely in the United States.

Ahmad Almallah grew up in Bethlehem, Palestine, and moved to the US when he was 18 years old. He is a poet, scholar, and translator of Arabic literature. His poems have appeared in *Jacket 2, Track/Four, All Roads Will Lead You Home, Apiary, Supplement,* and *SAND Journal.* His book *Bitter English* is forthcoming from the University of Chicago Press.

Hajer Almosleh—breaker of all stereotypes, warrior without making an effort. Mother of four grown-up fierce women in their 20's. Marathon runner, actress, translator, writer, lover, traveler, outspoken feminist, divorced and amicable, generous, supportive of the arts, bare back and arms, brown skin on white, smelling of nature and trees.

Omar Alsayyed, who was born in Jordan to an Egyptian-Palestinian family, grew up in Cairo and studied in New York City. He was a musician in *Shenandoah* at the Prague Fringe Festival and recently performed in *Malja'86*, a play set in the aftermath of the Lebanese Civil War.

Sinan Antoon is an Iraqi-born poet, novelist, scholar, and translator. He has published four novels and two collections of poetry. His works have have been translated into twelve languages. *The Book of Collateral Damage* is forthcoming from Yale University Press in 2019.

Ruth Awad is a Lebanese-American poet and the author of *Set to Music a Wildfire*, winner of the 2016 Michael Waters Poetry Prize from Southern Indiana Review Press.

Zeina Azzam is a Palestinian-American writer, editor, poet, and activist. She volunteers for organizations that promote Palestinian human rights and civil rights of vulnerable communities in Alexandria, Virginia, where she lives. Zeina holds an M.A. in Arabic literature.

Ibtisam Barakat is a Palestinian-American poet and author of award-winning books in English and Arabic, including *Tasting the Sky: A Palestinian Childhood; Balcony on the Moon: Coming of Age in Palestine*; and *Al-Ta Al-Marboota Tateer*.

Nora M. Barghati was born to a Libyan father and an American mother, and spent her childhood and early adulthood in Libya. In 2012, she moved to Kurdistan, where she is now residing with her husband and two boys.

Zeina Hashem Beck is a Lebanese poet. Her most recent collection, *Louder than Hearts*, won the 2016 May Sarton NH Poetry Prize. Her work has been widely published in literary magazines; her poem "Maqam" won *Poetry* magazine's 2017 Frederick Bock Prize.

Jehan Bseiso is a Palestinian poet and researcher who has been working with Médecins sans Frontières/Doctors Without Borders since 2008. Her co-authored book *I Remember My Name* (2016) is the creative category winner of the Palestine Book Awards.

Hayan Charara is the author of three poetry books, most recently, *Something Sinister*, winner of the Arab American Book Award. He is also series editor, with Fady Joudah, of the Etel Adnan Poetry Prize.

Baha' Ebdeir is a refugee living in Bethlehem, Palestine, originally from the occupied village of Bayt Nattif. He is studying at al-Quds Bard College, majoring in human rights and English literature.

Sharif S. Elmusa, a widely-published poet, scholar, and translator, is the author of the poetry collection *Flawed Landscape* and co-editor with Greg Orfalea of *Grape Leaves: A Century of Arab America*. Elmusa grew up in the refugee camp of al-Nuway'mah, near the ancient town of Jericho, Palestine.

Mohsen Emadi was born in northern Iran. His poetry appeared in numerous magazines as a young adult. He lived in Finland, the Czech Republic, and Spain before moving to Mexico, working as a lecturer and researcher in poetry and comparative literature. The author of seven collections of poetry, Emadi has had his work translated into many languages, including Spanish, English, French, and Arabic.

Angela Farmer is a poet and a revered elder yogini who has a yoga studio with her husband Victor Van Kooten on the island of Lesvos, Greece, near the beaches where tens of thousands of refugees landed from 2015–2017. From this location she had the privilege of welcoming families as they arrived. Angela teaches worldwide and with Victor in Lesvos.

Fouad Mohammed Fouad is a physician-poet from Aleppo. He and his family left Syria in 2012. He is now at the American University of Beirut. He has published five collections of poetry in Arabic. Several of his poems are translated into English and have been published in leading UK journals such as *Poem* and *Magma*.

Marisa Frasca is a poet, translator, book reviewer, and the author of *Via Incanto: Poems from the Darkroom*. Born in Vittoria Italy, Frasca resides on Long Island, New York.

Bronwen Griffiths is a published novelist, poet, and flash fiction writer. She works as a volunteer for Syria UK and lives in East Sussex.

Marilyn Hacker is the author of thirteen books of poems, most recently *A Stranger's Mirror* (Norton, 2015), an essay collection, *Unauthorized Voices* (Michigan, 2010), and numerous translations.

Golan Haji is a Syrian Kurdish poet and translator who now lives in Paris. His latest poetry collection, *A Tree Whose Name I Don't Know,* was published by A Midsummer Night's Press (New York, 2017). His most recent translation into Arabic is Alberto Manguel's *Packing My Library* (Dar al-Saqi, Beirut, 2018).

Nathalie Handal's most recent book, the flash collection *The Republics,* is the winner of the Virginia Faulkner Award for Excellence in Writing and the Arab American Book Award. Nathalie is a professor at Columbia University and writes the literary travel column The City and the Writer for *Words without Borders.*

Fatma Al Hassan is from Damascus, Syria. She is a teacher, writer, painter, and mother. After over a year waiting with six of her children in Elpida, a refugee camp in Thessaloniki, Greece, she joined her husband and two other children in Germany. She lives every day as a new adventure.

Merna Ann Hecht, poet, storyteller, and essayist, founded the Stories of Arrival: Refugee and Immigrant Youth Voices Poetry Project. She has worked for years with youth facing trauma and loss.

Zoe Holman is an Australian-British journalist, writer, scholar, and activist, specializing in the Arab Middle East. She is currently based in Athens, where she works with refugees.

Fady Joudah has published four collections of poems, including *The Earth in the Attic, Alight, Textu,* and *Footnotes in the Order of Disappearance.* He lives with his family in Houston where he practices internal medicine.

Mohja Kahf is the author of *The Girl in the Tangerine Scarf, E-Mails from Scheherazad, Hagar Poems,* and *Western Representations of the Muslim Woman: From Termagant to Odalisque.* She is a professor at the University of Arkansas, and since 2011 has been a member of the Syrian Nonviolence Movement.

Abu Bakr Khaal is an Eritrean novelist living in Denmark. He published *African Titanics* (2008), which was originally written in Arabic and translated into English in 2014 under the same title.

Lisa Suhair Majaj is the author of *Geographies of Light,* winner of the 2008 Del Sol Press Poetry Prize. Her poetry, prose, and critical essays have been published worldwide. Her poetry was included in the 2016 exhibit "Aftermath: The Fallout of War—America and the Middle East" at the Harn Museum of Art, University of Florida.

Khaled Mattawa currently teaches in the graduate creative writing program at the University of Michigan. His latest book of poems is *Tocqueville* (New Issues). A MacArthur Fellow, he is the current editor of the *Michigan Quarterly Review.*

Mootacem Bellah Mhiri teaches Arabic language and literature at Vassar College in New York and holds a doctorate in comparative literature from Penn State University.

Adele Ne Jame teaches poetry at Hawaii Pacific University. She has published four books of poems including *The South Wind* (2011) and has received numerous awards including a National Endowment for the Arts in Poetry, an Elliot Cades Award for Literature and a Robinson Jeffers Tor House Prize for poetry.

Naomi Shihab Nye, daughter of Aziz Shihab, born in Jerusalem in 1927. His last book was *Does the Land Remember Me? A Memoir of Palestine*, which was published by Syracuse University Press three months before his death in 2007. "Her own most recent book is *Voices in the Air: Poems for Listeners* (Greenwillow, 2018)."

Sara Abou Rashed was called "an inspiration" by Children's Defense Fund President Marian Wright Edelman. At 13 years old, she moved to the US, and at 16, Sara gave a TEDx Talk and was nominated for a Pushcart Prize. She was awarded the 2016 Denison Book Award and is currently a sophomore, pursuing International Studies and Narrative Journalism at Denison University.

Sara Saleh is a Palestinian-Egyptian-Lebanese artist, writer, and campaigner for refugee rights and racial justice based in Sydney, Australia. Sara's first poetry collection was released in August 2016, and she was recently featured in the Palestinian anthology, *A Blade of Grass.* Sara continues to perform nationally and internationally.

Abbas Sheikhi is an Iranian poet who traveled by raft with his daughter and pregnant wife to Lesvos, Greece. He and his wife studied English and volunteered at Khora, a refugee center in Athens, as a Farsi interpreter with Lawyers without Borders. They now live in Landau, Germany. "Here spring comes / green grasses / cover ground / colorful flowers / come out of the grass / dew sits on their calyxes / and wash their faces / the birds sing songs / say life is beautiful / and just one time / I say to myself / I don't miss it / yes everything / is beautiful / but here, is not my home."

Sanaa Shuaibi is from Deir ez Zor, Syria. She was the founder of a school for children in Syria, but had to leave because of the war. She lived in Greece for more than a year with her youngest daughter and husband, hoping to join their five children in Germany. Her paintings and poems were exhibited in a museum in Thessaloniki, Greece, in 2017.

Fadwa Suleiman was a well-known theater and film actor in Syria who left her career to be a spokesperson for what she hoped would be a democratic revolution. She became a political exile in 2012 and published her first book of poems, كلّما بلغ القمر., from which this sequence is taken, in 2013. Fadwa died of cancer in Paris in August 2017.

Becky Thompson, Ph.D., is a writer, poet, human rights activist, and professor. She is the author of multiple books, most recently, *Teaching with Tenderness* and the poetry collection *Zero is the Whole I Fall into at Night*. Since 2015 Becky has been traveling to Greece, meeting rafts, documenting human rights violations, and teaching poetry workshops.

Lena Khalaf Tuffaha is an American poet of Palestinian, Syrian, and Jordanian heritage. She is the author of *Water & Salt,* published by Red Hen Press (2017), winner of the 2018 Washington State Book Award, and *Arab in Newsland*, winner of the 2016 Two Sylvias Press Chapbook Prize. She lives with her family in Redmond, Washington.

Sholeh Wolpé was born in Iran. The inaugural 2018 Writer-in-Residence at UCLA, her literary work to date numbers over 12 collections of poetry, translations, and anthologies, as well as several plays.

Rewa Zeinati is a poet, writer, educator, and the founding editor of *Sukoon* magazine.

Reprint Acknowledgments

The following previously appeared in other works:

Antoon, Sinan, "Afterwords," *Letters to Palestine*, Vijay Prashad, ed. (London: Verso, 2015).

Awad, Ruth. "My Father, Is the Sea, the Field, the Stone" *Set to Music a Wildfire* (Evansville, Indiana: Southern Indiana Review Press, 2017).

Azzam, Zeina. "Leaving My Childhood Home." The Quarry: A Social Justice Poetry Database. Split This Rock, February 2016. http://www.splitthisrock.org/poetry-database/poem/leaving-my-childhood-home

Barakat, Ibtisam. "My People's Story," *Balcony on the Moon: Coming of Age in Palestine* (New York: Macmillan Publishing Group, Farrar, Straus, And Giroux Books for Young Readers, 2016).

Beck, Zeina Hashem. "Ghazal: Back Home" and "Naming Things" *Louder than Hearts* (New Hampshire: Bauhan Publishing, 2017).

Elmusa, Sharif. "An Update of our Fall," and "I Want my House to Stand," www.Jadaliyya.com/details/32472/ An-Update-of-our-Fall, September 20, 2015.

Emadi, Mohsen. "It is Snowing Outside…" *Standing on Earth*, Phoneme Media, USA, 2016.

Frasca, Marisa. "Under the Sky of Lampedusa, *Voices in Italiana Literary Journal* (New York: Bordighera Press, 2016).

Hacker, Marilyn. "Nieces and Nephews" in *Plume Poetry Anthology* 5, 2016 and PN Review (UK).

Haji, Golan. "To My Youngest Sister," "To Raed Naqshabandi," "To Akkad Nizam ad-Din," "To Mohammed Samy al-Kayyâl," "To Ruwa Riché," *Mizan Al-Adha (Scale of Injury)*, (Milan: al-Mutawassit, 2016).

Handal, Nathalie, "Beit" and "Heartsong," *The Invisible Star* (Valparaiso. 2014).

Majaj, Lisa Suhair. "Exile, Edge," *Matter: A (somewhat) monthly journal of political poetry and commentary*. https://mattermonthly.com/2016/04/27/exile-edge/ (2016).

Rashed, Sara Abou. "Welcome to America" appeared as "For America," *Pudding Magazine*, Fall 2016.

Tuffaha, Lena Khalaf, "Fragment," Broadsided Press, November 2015.

Wolpé, Sholeh. "The Outsider," *Rooftops of Tehran* (Pasadena, CA: Red Hen Press, 2008).